RIVALRY OF SUPREMACY

A NEW APPROACH TO ENJOYING POETRY

FRANCIS A. OGBE

ISBN-9798594501744
ISBN-9798594501744

Cover design by: 2D Media Production Studios
+234 816 6431 219

This book is dedicated to my sweetheart-Enny the Poet.

CONTENTS

FOREWORD

The existence of humanity underscores the meaning of life. Indeed, life is magnified by living it to its possible fullest, as many factors in turn collaborate with, or even conspire to determine the essence of living. These factors may include but are not limited to issues of survival, supremacy, love, conflict, spirituality, politics and intellectualism. It is the interplay of such indices that give life complexion and indeed the world an identity.

Yet, there is a constant debate as to the true essence of life. These daily dialogues oscillate from the metaphysical to the physical realist realm. Interestingly, the creative arts particularly literature has over the years taken centre stage in this sustainable discourse to evaluate life and its purpose. Hence, 'Rivalr of Supremacy' emerges as a veritable tool for the interpretation of life through the lens of poetry.

Thus, in his attempt to reconcile the basic complexities that inform our everyday relationships and interactions as human beings, from our homes to work places, our secular to spiritual livelihoods, the author romantcizes with reoccuring notions and emotions that shape our everyday life, using simple languages and common imagery to bring to fore common everyday issues that confront our shared humanity. Also instructive is the author's strong believe in the supremacy of the supernatural.

The lucid lyricism of Rivalry of Supremacy evokes so much simplicity of language and imagery, such that betrays the author's hidden passion for elementary poetry, one borne of clarity and ease of comprehension for the "ordinary man or woman " in the street. He wonders why poetry should be shrouded in any mystery when it's primary intent is to interpret life and its complexities. Simply put, this is simple poetry, laced in common dictionand presented in the most audacious yet elementary context.

At a time when our country stand at cross- roads pondering its existential realities and survival, the role of poetry as a vehicle for national rebirth and restructuring can never be over emphasized. It is a matter of fact, a moral obligation and patriotic call to service to mother land. And to this end, poets like the author, must rise to the occasion as forebearers to preach the gospel of nationalism through the barrel of the pen. This is what the author has achieved and most succintly too, in everyday simple language.

In this work, Francis Ogbe has succeeded in serving his audience a sumptuous cocktail of poems which provide a vital contributiuon to the sustainable national discourse menu but most particularly to literary scholarship. His painstaking enquiry and readable poetry all conspire to make his collection a required reading for students of poetry. It constitutes a standard reference volume for students of literature and lay readers alike.

Terna-Kester Kyenge PhD
Former parliamentarian and Lecturer

PROLOGUE

The collection "Rivalry of Supremacy: A New Approach To Enjoying Poetry" looks at various issues ranging from love, betrayal, rivalry, work place politics, spirituality and some national issues. Others are everyday home challenges like tenants and landlord relationship and poverty issues.

TO THE ONE I LOVE is simply a man's admiration and celebration of his spouse. His spouse is everything to him. She is as fair as the moon, bright as the sun and majestic as the stars in procession. This is the kind of love that young people see and the desire to fall in love. But the question is should VALENTINE'S DAY determines one's love for the other? Relationships have been broken because of Valentine. Oh poor Valentine! SEARCHING FOR GOLD captures the ordeal young men go through in trying to woo the love of their life. All men I suppose have their stories to tell good, bad or the ugly. Have you ever taken time to observe carefully couples on their WEDDING DAY? Waoh! It is always glorious! The couples booming in smiles, looking radiant, scintlating and charming. That's the dream of every unmarried adults especially spinsters. However, OH WHAT A FEELING is a dilemma of a young lady trapped in marriage. Not too sure of her matrimonial feelings, she is optimistic that the future is brighter between her spouse and her.

The ways of man are mysterious who can understand him? You give a kiss when you want to strike, oh what a deceit. The Poems OH MAN! and SO YOU LATER BETRAYED ME reveals the intricacies and dynamics of betrayals. Betrayal in the home front, in relationships, in the market place, in politics, even in the church.

I believe in spirituality! I believe in the supernatural! I believe the spiritual controls the physical! We all believe there is a supreme being up there. FOR THIS GOD IS MY GOD is an attempt at describing this BEING up there. The persona personalizes this God as 'my God' and enumerates his wonderous deeds in the affairs of men from time immemorial. THE PRAYER OF A TROUBLED MAN explains itself as it is a call to the Most High to deliver the persona from the troubles of life. In the poem COVENANT LIFE, we see a different persona who knows so he declares, 'I am a covenant child and I have a covenant life'. Similar to the' prayer of a troubled man' TAKE ME HIGHER is a call for divine help for vain is the help of man. There is a formula that no one can do without it is called ALMIGHTY FORMULA. What is it? How do you feel when your dream seems delayed? Your goals seem unachievable? And God seems to be silent? That is the story of SILENT GOD.

Life offers each of us different opportunities and experiences and most often, we tend to wonder why? why? why? LIFE IS NOT FAIR captures man's attempt at understanding life the four letter word. Closely related to the poem above is the poem on PROBLEMS. Every man detests them, they show up when you least expect them and stay much longer than you want them. The poem JOS is prophetic in nature as it captures the city of Jos yesterday, today and tomorrow. THE MYSTERY OF FAILURE will blow your min as it brings a new dimension and perspective to the narrative on failure. It is amazing to see MR AND MRS BUSY ever busy but unfortunately going no where as though they were on a treadmil. On the contrary are individuals who keep putting forward their assignment until their ship eventually become hardship. The solution to PROCRASTINATION is do it now. Here are three secrets for anyone who wants to be at the top of his or her game. First, life is all about ATTITUDE.Poor attitude poor results and great attitude great results.Secondly, dare to dream (IMAGINATION) , allow your imagination to fly. Thirdly, all great men are men of SOLITUDE for great ideas are birthed in solitude. How painful it is to see life being stuffed away from your loved one because you couldn't afford the hospital bill. The poem POVERTY exposes the evils of poverty and challenges the reader to find an escape route because there is nothing glorifying about poverty. As you gradually climb the ladder of success, BECAREFUL WHO HELP YOU because some helps are better rejected than accepted.

In an attempt to make ends meet, we sometimes accept employment that is not our dream job. ZARIA ACADEMY reveals a persona who believes Zaria Academy is not his final destination. What are you actually looking for? A job or work? Which is better- job or work? THE SLAVERY OF A JOB provides the answer. THANK GOD IT'S FRIDAY? It's a lament of a worker or group of workers who have been condemned to work on every weekend. However, they are hopeful that one day, they will be able to say thank God it's friday. I have worked in the media for some years now and one thing that baffles me is THE RIVALRY between News and Programmes Directorate. It is like the age long rivalry between Romeo and Julieth's family. You are told how glorious the job of a TD is but the reality on ground betrays what you are told. THE TD AND THE MCR gives you a glimpse into the workings of a television house.

It is a terrible experience if you fall into the hands of a wrong HOUSE AGENT but the question begging for answer is who makes a better agent men or women? Closely related is another poem titled GOD

BLESS MY LANDLORD which is a tribute to a landlord encountered by the persona. The persona reveals what makes this landlord different from other landlords. Everybody wants FREEDOM but not all know the true meaning of freedom. No greater burden than freedom, no heavier load than freedom. KOOM AND THE KEYBOARD is a mixture of admiration, celebration, warning and advice to Brother Koom. SELECTIVE JUSTICE is applicable everywhere either at home, in the work place, in the market even in the church. Why are rules administerd on just a few and not all? THE MIRACLE BUDGET x-rays the unrealistic hope of the 2016 budget that was believed to solve all the problems in the nation. How true is this? MY COUNTRY MY COUNTRY could be likened to a sitcom titled 'Fuji House of Commotion'. Everyday with unimaginable tales and fallacies only in MY COUNTRY.

COVID-19 LOCKDOWN is an attempt at capturing the hydraheaded pandemic that has brought the world to it's knees. And ODE TO MY DG is a tribute by the persona to his DG for his milk of human kindness.

This is the author's attempt at making poetry easy to comprehend.

TO THE ONE I LOVE

How beautiful you are my darling!
Oh how beautiful!
Your love is more delightful than wine,
Pleasing is the fragrance of your perfume.
Your name is like perfume poured out.
You are dark, yet lovely and beautiful.
My lover is to me a sachet of myrrh,
You are my rose of Sharon
The Lily of my Valley
You are my ORENTE!

Your eyes are Doves,
Your cheeks are beautiful,
Your lips drop sweetness as the honey comb.
Your neck adorned with strings of jewels,
Your graceful legs with the smoothness of a toddler,
Your statue is like that of the palm-tree,
The work of a craftsman's hand,
You are a wonder to behold.

You have stolen my heart oh! my darling,
My darling, you who appears like the Dawn,
Fair as the Moon,
Bright as the Sun,
Majestic as the Stars in procession,
How beautiful you are my darling,
Oh! How beautiful!

VALENTINE

Before Valentine I love you,
Without Valentine I still love you,
Valentine can't determine my love for you,
Neither can it break my love for you.
You have found a special place in my heart,
You are so dear and precious to me,
Who and what can separate me from your love?
Can Valentine separate you from my love?
With or without Valentine,
We are meant for each other.
Before the foundation of creation,
We are destined for each other,
Our love is like the unbreakable rock of Jubrata,
Remember, I never fell in love with you,
I only grew in love with you.
Those who fall in love always fall out of love,
But for you we grow in love,
Even without Valentine.
It all started like a little drop of water,
I can see it welling into an ocean of love,
With or without Valentine,

I love you affectionately.

SEARCHING FOR GOLD

Searching for a life partner,
Is like searching for gold.
It is like searching for a pin in a deep ocean.
It is like an adventure to an unknown land.
It is like searching for a lost coin under the cover of darkness.
Always searching and ever searching,
That one day you will find it.

Searching for a life partner,
Is like searching for gold in the mines.
It is not always easy,
You despise the shame, the ridicule and the disappointments.
No matter the disappointments,
You are determined to wait,
Because you are searching for something precious,
Your missing rib.

**Searching for a life partner,
Is like the Gulder's ultimate search,
So many abortive appointments,
Yet not discouraged.
Always hopeful,
That it is going to be well.
For nothing good comes easy,
Especially the job of searching for your Gold,
Your precious and adorable Jewel.**

WEDDING DAY

There are three events in the life of a man,
The day of his Birth,
The day of his Death,
The day of his Wedding.
While others celebrate the first two on his behalf,
He is only opportune to witness one-
The day of his wedding.
How wonderful it is on the day of one's Wedding.
The Couple all booming in smiles,
Looking cheerful,
Radiant, scintillating, charming,
Waoh! Waoh!! Waoh!!!
The lady looking more beautiful,
Than the first day you opened up to her.
That day is always a memorable day,
Everyone dreams to see it happen in his/her life,
Or are you destined for the seminary or convent?

OH WHAT A FEELING!!!

Is this what it takes to be happy?
Am I really happy?
Should I say I am?
Is this a mixed feeling?
Why am I depressed?
Why am I worried?
Why are my eyes filled with tears?
Why the alteration in my sleeping pattern?
Should I say am suffering for the sin of another person?
Is that what I get as a reward Lord?
No..................
What a feeling.............!!!

This has been my worry and fears from the onset,
Is this what it takes when you happen not to be the first lover?
Am I a victim or a victor in the whole scenario?
Am I thinking right?
Am I assuming the whole incidence?
Oh Lord show me your mercy and favour,

Am I going beyond my boundary in the home?
Am I in the right place?
I guess I am.
Then why does my heart ache sometimes when lonely?
Why this feeling of pain in the inside?
Oh! What a feeling...........?

Am I really appreciated for who I am?
Am I even welcome?
My head aches!
Why do I feel like withdrawing from myself?
Oh Lord help me!
Let not my enemies' triumph over me,
I know this feeling is just for a while,
Oh Lord! Help me to overcome these unusual feelings,
I refuse to be discouraged,
I know my redeemer liveth,
The future is brighter between my spouse and I,
Oh, what a feeling!!

OH MAN!!!

Man, oh man!
Who can understand you?
Your ways are mysterious
Who can understand you?
Man, your heart is full of deceit
Who can understand you?
You strike when no one expect you
Who can understand you?
You smile when you mean hate
Who can understand you?
You give a kiss when you want to strike
Who can understand you?
Man, oh man!
You are like deep waters.

SO, YOU LATER BETRAYED ME!!!

Oh, my best friend!
The one I trust whole heartedly,
The one with whom I shared my food,
Has suddenly turned against me.
I remember that scorching afternoon I visited you,
Yes, it was on the Lord's Day,
How you spoke gently, friendly and sickly to me,
But I never knew you were planning evil in your heart.
Why did you do this to me?
So, you later betrayed me!

Oh, my best friend!
You could have told me your heart.
I could have prepared for your coming,
But no, you decided to build my hope on high.
You allowed it to reach the crescendo,
And when I thought my dream was becoming fruitful,

You suddenly appeared in the scene,
Dashed away my hopes,
And let me down like a bag of cement,
So, you later betrayed me!

Oh, my best friend!
If an enemy had done this to me,
I could have borne it.
Instead it was you-
My equal, my companion and my close friend.
The one we fellowshipped together,
The one who was under my leadership,
Has suddenly turned against me.
Though looking guiltless,
But you later betrayed me.

Oh, my best friend!
Why did you use me to achieve your ambition?
Thus, causing delay and setbacks on my own goals.
However, I still believe in the God of divine speed,
But I ask again, why did it take you long to let me know your intentions?
You could have told me when I came to bid you welcome,
But you kept mute and pretended all was well,
Until that 'GOOD FRIDAY'
When I was court martialed and given the final Verdict,
And you later betrayed me.

Oh, my best friend!
You made me look devilish
Before the small world.
Even my closest acquaintances doubted my Integrity and credibility.
Only few gave me words of encouragement to brace up to this trial in good fate.
I became like a lone voice,
No one really believed me.
Your act really pierced me deep into my bone marrow,
And I wondered why? Why? Why?
Why did you later betray me?

Oh, my best friend!
Why did you later betray me?
And the agreement we had on the Lord's Day?
Though just the both us,
The unseen guest was in our midst.
Don't you fear him?
Very soon the Cork will Crow,
Then all those in our small world,
Will know who is who,

But my friend, you later betrayed me.

Oh, my friend!
You played the fool of me.
No, not really,
I was only been disobedient to my father,
Who allowed me to have a taste of my disobedience,
I ignored the words of elders,
And was unable to overcome your scheme.
But he has promised to restore my fortune,
But I still wonder,
Why you later betrayed me.

Oh, my best friend!
My father has always told me,
Son, it is better to trust in me,
Than to put your confidence in your powerful friends'.
I never listened,
I wanted to try my strength and ingenuity,

Until you came into my life with your acts
And proved the authenticity of my father's words,
Thanks for that revelation,
But you later betrayed me!

Oh, my best friend!
Congratulations!
The deed has been done,
But you can't escape the impartial judgement
We are both waiting for our vindication,
From the one who is invisible,
But whose works are visible,
The righteous Judge,
But I ask again why?
Why did you later betray me?

Oh, my best friend!
May the unseen guest on that Sabbath day of our agreement,
Pay the guilty one the punishment he so richly deserves,
Pay the unfaithful friend in proportion to his wickedness.
Let the agreement breaker have a taste-
A taste of the evil he has done to the other.
But I ask again,
Why? Why? Why? Why.........?
Why did you do this to me?
So, you later betrayed me!!!

FOR THIS GOD IS MY GOD

For this God, is my God;
Which God?
The God that the Mountains saw and skipped like a ram,
The God that the Red Sea saw and parted ways,
The God that the Jordan saw and fled like a Mouse,
The God that is terrible in praises,
This God will be my guide unto the end.

For this God is my God,
Which God?
The God that walketh upon the Sea,
The God that maketh a way in the Wilderness,
The God that provideth water in the Desert,
The God that brought water out of the Rocks,
This God will be my guide unto the end.

For this God is my God,

Which God?
The God that specializes in impossible cases,
The God that is higher than the highest,
The God that is greater than the greatest,
The God that cuts the bars of iron asunder,
This God will be my guide unto the end.

For this God is my God,
Which God?
The God that supplieth Coconut water,
The God that shut the Lion's mouth,
The God that killeth and maketh alife,
The God that created the Heavens, the Earth and its
inhabitants,
This God will be my guide unto the end.

THE PRAYER OF A TROUBLED MAN!

I am in trouble!
My eyes are consumed with grief,
My soul and belly are as well consumed,
My life is spent with grief,
My strength fails me,
My enemies laugh and make jest of me,
My neighbours spare me not their ridicule,
They ask "where is the God you serve"?
Oh God arise!
Arise and deliver me speedily,
I am like a broken vessel,
I am forgotten as a dead man out of mind,
Arise and deliver me,
My times and seasons are in your hands!!!

COVENANT LIFE

I am a covenant Child,
I am a destiny Child,
I live a covenant life,
Because your covenants are tested and trusted.
They are dependable,
My maker is a covenant keeper,
His covenant will he not break,
Nor alter the words that have gone out of his mouth.
For this reason, I have made a covenant with my eyes,
Never to look at a woman /man lustfully.

I am a covenant child,
I am a destiny child,
My friends wonder why I am different.
Evil doers are perturbed why I don't walk in the way of sinners
Nor sit in the seat of scornful,
Neighbours know there is something unique about me,
It is because I live a covenant life.

I am a covenant child,
I am a destiny child,
Covenant people don't go everywhere,
Covenant people don't talk anyhow,
Covenant people don't dress anyhow,
Because they are bound by covenant,
They know the terms of the covenant,
That they are the utmost beneficiaries of the covenant.

I am a covenant child,
I am a destiny child,
What about you?
Do you live a covenant life?
Do you have a covenant?
With whom do you have a covenant?
The Most High is my covenanter,
And I am his covenantee.

TAKE ME HIGHER!

Oh Lord take me higher!
Higher than where I have ever been,
Higher than my wildest imagination,
There is a place I long to be,
Only you can take me there,
Above the expectations of my foes.
Let not my enemies rejoice over me,
Take me higher to the rock that is higher than I,
For I am meant for the top,
I believe in God,
God believes in me.
Take me higher to the next level,
Lord, I mean the next level,
Oh Lord take me higher!

ALMIGHTY FORMULA

The Devil frowns when we kneel to pray,
He trembles when we lift up our hands to pray,
He cries when we begin to pray,
Common people do not pray they only beg.
Wishing will never be a substitute for prayer,
Prayer time is never wasted time,
Prayer is an avenue for the meeting of humanity and divinity,
It is not a monologue but dialogue.
Prayer alone proves that you trust God,
God governs the world,
Prayer governs God,
Prayer the master key,
Prayer settles every equation,
Have you tried the Almighty formula today?

SILENT GOD

When God seems silent in the affairs of your life,
When you wonder why?
When you think you have done your part in all ramifications,
And God seems silent,
Still trust in Him.
Though it's not easy,
Learn to trust in Him,
Learn to hold on to Him until you breathe your last,
I will wait on Him until my change comes.

When God seems silent,
And your dream seems to be delayed,
Your goal seems unachievable,
You call on the one you know,
And God seems to be silent.
You ask questions,
And God seems to be silent.
You knock at the door,
And God seems to be silent.

You seek all round,
And God seems to be silent.
And you wonder why? Why? Why?
And God still seems to be silent.

You even question his faithfulness,
And doubt his existence,
You ask,
Is God still there?
Is God still watching?
Is God still alive?
When has He become a deaf and dumb God?
For how long will I wait?
I feel his absence more than his presence.
Oh God will you not speak?
Will you not just say a word to me?

LIFE IS NOT FAIR!!!

Life! Life!! Life!!!
This four letter word,
What is life?
What is the meaning of life?
Life is mysterious,
Life is not a linear plot,
It is an episodic plot,
It is full of twists, turns, ups and downs,
Alas! these are elements that make life interesting,
Notwithstanding, life is not fair!

Life! Life!! Life!!!
What is life?
What is the meaning of life?
Life offers each of us different opportunities,
No one has it all,
No one knows it all,
When you wonder why?
How one person graduates at the age of twenty,

Struggles for five years,
Gets a job at the age of twenty-five.
Another graduate at the age of twenty-five,
Gets a job immediately.
Haba! Why?
Am sure you will say destiny,
But life is not fair!

Life! Life!! Life!!!
What is life?
What is the meaning of life?
When you wonder why?
One marries a virgin,
Waits for a decade before becoming a father.
Another marries a prostitute,
Probably with series of abortion,
Becomes a happy mother of children immediately.
Life why?
How do you explain that?
Life is not fair!

Lif e! Life!! Life!!!
What is life?
What is the meaning of life?
When you wonder why?
How one becomes a Managing Director at the age of thirty-five,
Dies at fifty-five.
Another becomes a Managing Director at the age of fifty-five,
Enjoys life till ninety.

Why?
What is the meaning of life?
Life is not fair!

Life! Life!! Life!!!
What is life?
What is the meaning of life?
When you wonder why?
Godly parents,
With promiscuous children,
Wayward parents,
With godly children.
Life why?
What happened?
Life is not fair!

Life! Life!! Life!!!
What is life?
What is the meaning of life?
So many unanswered questions,
Why this?
Why that?
Oh God!
Get set for my arrival,
We shall meet face to face,
We shall slug it out,
I will not take no for an answer,
Life is not fair!

Life! Life!! Life!!!
What is life?
What is the meaning of life?
I can hear a lone voice,
Crying in the wilderness,
God never promises an easy road,
But he promised his everlasting presence.
He never promises **IF,**
But he promised **WHEN.**
I beg your pardon,
Remember Job?
Do you want to question God?
Not at all,
But life is not fair!

Life! Life!! Life!!!
What is life?
What is the meaning of life?
I can hear a lone voice,
Crying in the wilderness,
Not of him that runneth,
Not of him that willeth,
It is of God that showeth mercy.
But Oh God!
Life is not fair!

Life! Life!! Life!!!
What is life?

What is the meaning of life?
I can hear the lone voice,
Crisp and clearer,
Crying in the wilderness,
Not by power,
Not by might,
But by my spirit,
Do you want to question my authority?
Not at all,
All I am saying,
Life is not fair?

Life! Life!! Life!!!
What is life?
What is the meaning of life?
I can hear the lone voice,
Louder than a megaphone,
Crying in the wilderness,
In the race of life,
Our tracks are different,
Our timings are different,
No absolute finish line for all,
We only have a common umpire,
All right,
I rest my case.
Is life fair?

PROBLEMS!!!

Problems do not come alone but in pairs,
They book no appointment,
They have no regard for Age, Class, Religion or Tribe.
They are like uninvited guest,
They stay much longer than you want them to,
Everyman detest them.
They show up when you least expect them,
They are man's Companion,
No man lives without them,
We are even encouraged to expect them,
The earlier we do, the better we become.
Attitude is all that matters.

II

Problems are the reason for every improvement we make,
Problems quicken our wit,
Problems stiffen our spine.
Problems force you to think outside the box,

Problems are opportunities to step into new dimension of accomplishment.
Problems awaken the giant in us,
Some describe it as the necessity of invention,
God sees it as promise-problem-provision.
Problems are inevitable but suffering is optional,
May your day be filled with problems,
Is that a good prayer?

JOS

Oh, my Jos!
Oh, my sweet Jos!
The home of Peace and Tourism,
The centre of Rocky Mountains,
The home of attraction,
For both the Blacks and the Whites.
Everyone wants to build on the Plateau,
God's own garden.
Jos-what a beauty to behold-
The water falls,
The carefully arranged rocks,
The wild lives,
To mention but a few.
Jos- the peak of God's architectural design.

Oh, my Jos!
Oh, my sweet Jos!
What has befallen you?
Oh, my sweet Jos.
Who has disfigured you?
Oh, my Jos.

Who has bewitched you?
Oh, my sweet Jos.
Who and what has impoverished you?
Oh, my Jos.
Who has torn your clothes into rags?
Oh, my sweet Jos.
Who are the perpetrators of this dastardly act?
Oh my Jos.
May nemesis catch up with them,
May the God of the Plateau expose them,
May their day be filled with thick darkness,
May their path be eternally slippery unto destruction.

Oh, my Jos!
Oh, my sweet Jos!
You that was once the pride of the nation,
You have been made a by-word on the lips of men.
You that was once the centre of attraction with beehives of tourist activities,
You are suddenly becoming desolate.
Oh, my sweet Jos!
You are gradually losing your beauty,
Who has done this evil to you?
What becomes the future of my sweet Jos?
Will Jos ever regain its pride of place again?

Oh, my Jos!
Oh, my sweet Jos!
I know you will rise again,

For every distinction is preceded by a distraction.
I see a new Jos springing up,
Whose glory and beauty transcend the former,
Jos will be highly lifted up,
To be seen by all and sundry.
Oh, my Jos!
Oh, my sweet Jos!
All men shall once again call you blessed,
Jos, my sweet home Jos!

THE MYSTERY OF FAILURE

Failure is a situation, an experience and not a personality,
It may look like a fact, but it is only an option.
Failure is an opportunity to learn something new,
It is also an opportunity to start all over more intelligently,
No success story without a taste of failure,
Ninety-nine percent of success is built on experienced failures.
Successful people have more failures in their lives than average people do,
It is better to fail doing something, than to excel at doing nothing.
People who have no failures have no victories,
People who are not making mistakes are not risking enough,
Failure can become a weight or it can give you wings to fly.
It can either be a bridge or a barricade,
God never sees you as a failure,
He sees you as a learner.

Learn your lesson from failure and forget the details,
Failure is not falling down but staying down,
You are not a failure, until you begin to blame somebody else.

MR. & MRS. BUSY

Everyone seems to be busy,
Everyone seems to be on the move,
People are moving forward,
Others are moving backward.
Some are moving sideways,

Others are even moving in circles,
But all seem to be heading nowhere,
As though they are on a treadmill.
Most people think the main goal of life is to stay busy.
Busy- Are you progressing?
Activity does not equal accomplishment,
This is a trap,
Mr. and Mrs. Busy,
To be forewarned is to be forearmed.

PROCRASTINATION

The time to act is now,
Tackle all difficulty now,
The longer you wait the bigger it grows.
What you put off until tomorrow, you will probably put off tomorrow.
There is nothing like tomorrow, tomorrow never exist.
When a procrastinator has finally made up his mind, the opportunity must have passed
Procrastinators are good at talking not doing,
People who sit around waiting for their ship, often delve into hardship.
Eliminate all excuses for not taking action,
Those who dodge responsibilities can't dodge its consequences,
Whatever is worth doing is worth doing now and well.
Someday, is not a day of the week,
Wasting time is wasting your life,
The solution to procrastination is do it now.

ATTITUDE

Life is all about attitude!
It controls your environment and your entire world.
Poor attitude poor result,
Great attitude great result.
Life is not so much a matter of position but disposition
It's your attitude not your aptitude.
Your attitude determines your altitude,
Attitude is the magic word.
While some see difficulty in every opportunity,
Others see opportunity in every difficulty.
It is all a function of attitude.
It is not what happens to you but what happens in you that matters,
You are in charge of your attitude,
Live everyday with an attitude of positive expectancy.

IMAGINATION

You were created for creativity,
Make a daily demand on your creativity.
Everything starts as somebody's daydream,
All great men are first dreamers.
Imagination has the power to light its own fire,
Ability is a flame, creativity is a blaze,
Allow your imagination to fly,
Allow your imagination to scale the walls of limitations.
Vision is seeing things others don't see,
It is seeing the impossible,
If you can see the invisible then you can do the impossible.
Vision keeps you going in life,
Dare to dream,
It cost you nothing to dream.

SOLITUDE

Great ideas are born in solitude,
Great men are made in secret places,
Great stories are written in solitude,
Great thinkers are men who love solitude.
Mediocres are crowd conscious people,
Lazy people fear solitude,
Dare to be alone,
Alone with God.
Alone with good books.
Eagles fly alone,
Other birds fly in group.
Believe in yourself,
Believe in God,
You and God make the best team.

POVERTY

Poverty, I passionately hate you,
Poverty, I dislike you,
You are the destroyer of destinies,
You have cut short the days of many,
You have rendered many useless.
So many unnecessary deaths in the hospital because of you,
You are the delayer of destiny,
Many have sold their birth right because of you,
Not because they want,
But because you have held them captive.

Since the day I was set loose from you,
I vow never to become your victim again.
I vow to launch an attack of prosperity against you,
I vow to destroy your stronghold on any member of my family.
I vow to cancel all the troubles you have brought on my family through poverty.
I declare you my enemy.

Through prosperity I will disgrace you,
Through prosperity you will be put to shame,
You will regret for ever letting me out of your net,

I will wreak havoc on you.
I will stir many against you,
Even your captives will revolt against you,
By the reason of the light they shall encounter,
You have held us bound for too long,
We have been deceived for too long that you are our friend,
That you are the best cross we can carry,
But today, a great light has shone upon our darkness,
That you are not a friend but a foe,
Today we rise against you vehemently Oh poverty!

You afflict the ignorant,
The oppressor of the ignorant,
Destroyer of the ignorant,
But woe to you.
You no longer have power over me,
I walk into my abundance today,
Today I walk into my prosperity,
I shake you off my life, destiny, future and family.
Through prosperity, I shall be established,
Through prosperity my fame shall spread abroad,
I fought poverty and I won.

BE CAREFUL WHO HELP YOU

Help is good,
It is a wonderful thing when one receives help,
You feel loved when help comes your way,
However, be careful who help you.

Some help can lead to enslavement,
Others can mar you.
Some help make you compromise,
Others make you lose your voice,
Therefore, be careful who help you.

Some help are better rejected than accepted,
Though it may be painful,
But learn to say no to some help,
Is it impossible?
Some help are detrimental,
Therefore, be careful who help you.

Some may help you and want to control your destiny,
Others help you to prove a point.
Some may help you to claim your achievement,
Others help you and threaten to withdraw their help.
May God deliver you from satanic help,
Only heaven's help is authentic,
Therefore, be careful who help you.

ZARIA ACADEMY

Oh, Zaria Academy!
Thank you for coming into my life,
You have given me momentary joy and happiness,
But I refuse to be satisfied.
I am going somewhere,
You are not my destination,
And cannot be my destination,
And will never be my destination.

I refuse to settle for average,
There are better things elsewhere,
It is just a matter of time.
I believe I can fly,
I believe I can still fly beyond your walls,
Oh, Zaria Academy!
You are only a thorough fare,
You are just a bus-stop before I reach my destination,
Oh, Zaria Academy!

THE SLAVERY OF A JOB

Do you have a job or a work?
Which is better- a job or a work?
A job may or may not employ your gifts and talents,
A job may provide a source of income not necessarily fulfillment,
A job may fill your life with activities not necessarily effectiveness,
A job might render you busy not progressive.

In a job you endure rather than enjoy
In a job you sit through hours of emotional and mental torture longing for closing time
In a job you may not find joy and fulfillment,
A job therefore becomes a glorified form of slavery for many.
A job also becomes a social prison,
And many become employed prisoners and slaves.

Adam was placed in the garden not to take a job but to Work,

Move beyond a job into your work.
Work provides an opportunity to release and expose your full potential,
Work occupies your time, talents, gifts and passion,
A Job without fulfillment is only a preoccupation and not an Occupation.

Are you willing to risk the safety of your job for the sake of a personal vision?
A personal vision that would have national and historic impact.
In a job, you only take from life,
In a work, you give to life to make an impact,
You only retire from a job not work,
May you be delivered from the Egyptian mentality of a job.

THANK GOD IT'S FRIDAY?

Thank God it's Friday!
Expectations are high,
Workers are in high spirit,
None wants to be held back in the office,
Frail nerves are gradually becoming calm,
Rising tempers are gradually rolling down,
Faces exude with smiles,
Everyone anxious to leave the office,
Thank God it's Friday.

Thank God it's Friday!
The day that ushers in a great weekend,
People are anxious to meet their love ones,
Spend quality time with special ones that work has put asunder,
Opportunity to travel,
Opportunity to party with friends,

Opportunity to be away from your quiet "killing" boss(es),
Dating appointments are fixed for the weekend,
Relationships are fixed for the weekend,
Thank God it's Friday.

Thank God it's Friday!
Workers want to get out of work pressured environment,
They want to go and unwind,
They want to freshen up,
Prepare for another brand-new week with vigour and vitality.
Everyone looks forward to it,
With enthusiasm and excitement,
Like a bride who waits for her groom,
Thank God it's Friday.
Alas! Not so for Weekly Diary producer(s),
The day a Weekly Diary producer fears most.

Thank God it's Friday!
Thank God it's Friday?
Not so for Weekly Diary producer(s),
No one looks forward to it,
It's like a dreaded Monster,
Ever frightful,
Always tortuous.
Never ending,
Gradually pulling you away from your creator,
No financial gain to show for it,

The pain is renewed every week,
Thank God it's Friday?

Thank God it's Friday!
Thank God it's Friday?
Not so for Weekly Diary producer(s),
It is the beginning of a tortuous weekend,
The beginning of a sleepless weekend,
Not in the comfort of your home,
But in your work pressured office.
Must it always be an all-night weekend?
Why casual at day and zealous at night?
Is it a game plan?
Is the programme cursed?
For how long will this continue?
Thank God it's Friday?

Thank God it's Friday!
Thank God It's Friday?
Not so for Weekly Diary producer(s),
All attempts to break the jinx of not sleeping have proved abortive,
Even younger redeemers have been held bound by the spell.
I think someone is benefitting from this weekend hostage,
I think some are scared of working during the day,
Others are scared of what the weekend holds,
So, they keep others with them in the dungeon.
Some are scared of being alone during weekends,

So, everyone must have two nights of the weekend
with them in the office.
Others I think want to impress their superiors,
But I know one day,
Weekly Diary Producer(s) will say
Thank God it's Friday!

THE RIVALRY

It is great fun working in a Television House,
It is even prestigious when it is a National Television,
It is most unimaginable when you are An On-Air Personality.
Friends and Foes believe you are made,
They put you in a class of your own,
You dare not complain of being "broke",
Or you are considered stingy,
Perception versus reality.

II

My name is ANGEL,
I just came back from the State,
My family home in Nigeria is like a Motor Park,
Filled with both near and distant relations.
I have a brother in Programmes Directorate.
A sister in News Directorate,
A cousin in Engineering Department,
An aunt in Finance Department,

An uncle in Tdmin and training,
And a nephew in Marketing Department.

III

This is the fifth year since I got back,
And there is something I have noticed,
The rivalry.
The rivalry between News and Programmes Directorate,
Have you ever noticed it?
It makes my heart bleed,
It is like an age long rivalry,
Like the rivalry between the Nigerian Medical Doctors and Nurses,
Like the rivalry between Romeo and Juliet's family,
Like the unending rivalries within the Ruling Party.

IV

The rivalry seems to have spread between my siblings,
It has even affected their siblings,
It is the same all over,
From Makurdi to Port-Harcourt,
From Jos to Ibadan,
From Kaduna to Enugu,
From Sokoto to Lagos,
And in the seat of Power-the ultimate Headquarters.

V

This rivalry is amazingly seen even in the recruited staff,
And one wonders why it is so?
It seems not to be in other Departments,
Why is it so in my brother and sister's Directorate?
More painfully,
It has been transferred to the home front,
Though I don't work there,
I can tell you all that happens there accurately,
I can even call names,
This is the extent of the rivalry even at home.

VI

It is the rivalry of supremacy,
Which often leads to arrogancy.
Which is better?
News or Programmes Directorate?
Who owns the air waves?
News or Programmes Directorate?
Which is more popular?
News or Programmes Directorate?
Which earns more money for the organization?
News or Programmes Directorate?

Which earns more money for the individual?
News or Programmes Directorate?
Which should step down for the other?
News or Programmes Directorate?
The list is endless,
And the answer seems to be obvious,
But I thought they say television is a team work,
Why the rivalry?
When will it end?

VII

From reliable sources,
Confirmed by my brother and sister,
Everybody wants to run to News Directorate,
Even the cleaner wants to be News Cleaner,
The security man wants to be News Directorate security man,
Amusing, the Driver wants to be News Driver,
Amazingly, authority gives special preference to news directorate,
Why others struggle with a car for their assignment,
News Directorate has more than three cars at their disposals,
Even the only car you have can be given to news if the need arises,
The reverse can never be the case.
When will this rivalry end?
Who can bring this rivalry to an end?

VIII

Don't you think there is something News Directorate is doing that others are not doing?
From observations,
Corroborated by my siblings,
News Directorate is more united than others,
Despite their internal Wrangling,
Their bosses appear more pragmatic than others,
Their bosses fight for its people than others,
They hardly accept faults like others,
Even when they are wrong,
Blame must always go to others,
This they do with all their strength and might.
They enjoy privileges others don't,
They enjoy air time others don't,
Their least event is well celebrated,
While others deny their people such opportunities,
Who wouldn't want to join such a group?

THE TD AND THE MCR

Working in a Television House is great fun,
Working in its Master Control Room (MCR) is greater fun,
Working as a Transmission Director (TD) is the greatest of all fun,
You are the gatekeeper,
Between the media house and the outer world.
Doesn't it feel great?
You can do and undo-Really?
You have the final say-Is it really true?
You are told how glorious the job is,
The reality on ground betrays what you are told,

Some consider it a job for nonentity,
Others are punished by been made a TD,
Many are considered too big for the job,
Would you want to be a TD?
Would you be delighted to remain a TD?

II

An excruciating pain the day you are punished,
Queried for what you consider a little mistake,
Are TD's above mistakes?
Despite your carefulness,
Blank appears on air,
And you are queried,
Even blown out of proportion,
By those who know little or nothing about it.
Past efforts are forgotten,
And you are almost nailed to the stake,
Would you want to be a TD?
Would you be delighted to remain a TD?

III

You play a scheduled tape,
And you are asked why the tape was played,
There is loss of audio in some parts of the track ups,
And you are given the threat of your life,
A respondent makes an unfriendly but true statement,
And you get queried to explain why?
And even threatened with "Aso Rock".
Would you want to be a TD?
Would you be delighted to remain a TD?

IV

Why is the TD blamed for everything?
Where are the Producers of such Programmes?
Where is the Quality Controller?
Where are the Librarians?
Where are the Engineers?
Why is the TD blamed for everything?
This is the plight of an average TD,
Working in an undigitized master control room (MCR),
Would you want to be a TD?
Would you be delighted to remain a TD?

HOUSE AGENT!

Different strokes for different folks,
Like a double edge sword,
You tell the story from the angle of the sword that has touched you.
Oh Agent!
Why are you so dubious?
Why is your conscience dead?
Why have you thrown away morality?
Why is sincerity far away from you?
Why can't you be trusted? Oh Agent!
Why are friends and neighbours angry with you whenever your name is mentioned?
Why must you knock heads of your clients together?
Why must you promise one building to two different persons?
Why mandatory payment of two- or three-year's house rent? Oh Agent!
Why do you find it difficult to refund fees even when the deal is not done?

Oh Agent!
Woe betide that Agent that eats other people's sweat,
Woe betide that Agent that reaps where he has not sown,
Woe betide that Agent that defrauds his client,
Are all Agents the same?
Alas, hurray! to that Agent who has been able to build his reputation on Credibility,
Great is that Agent who cherishes good name than polluted riches,
Bravo to that Agent whose friends and neighbours can vouch for,
Blessed is that Agent whose delight is the complete settlement of his client.
His reward is not only in the hereafter,
Clients will bless him,
Clients will recommend him to others,
His jar of oil will never run dry,
Clients will surround his business table,
His vine will never be fruitless,
As one drops, other sprouts out,
So great is the reward of that agent that is good and credible.

Oh Agent!
You can be credible if you want to be,
The choice is yours.
Remember, what goes around comes around,
The world is too small a place to be a cheat,
Oh Agent! be careful.
Who makes a better Agent?
A male or a female Agent?
Only time will tell.

GOD BLESS MY LANDLORD!

I

There is always a thin line between Agents and Landlords that is if any.
Landlords are known to be mean,
Landlords are known to be selfish,
Landlords are known to be greedy,
Landlords are known to be heartless.
These are the characteristics of Landlords we were made to know,
We grew up and discover them to be true.

II

However, my mentality changed when I fell into the hands of a young Landlord,
I guess my age mate,
With a beautiful wife, lovely kids and blessed with wonderful relations.
It all started the day I arrived my one-bedroom flat,

The Landlord's wife ran towards me, welcomed me and collected my bag,
I wondered at this gesture and concluded,
Perhaps, she woke up at the right side of her bed,
Alas! I was wrong.
Another shocker!
When I opened my flat I discover it has been washed by the Landlord and his family.
Again, I marveled and concluded,
They are trying to impress me,
Alas! I was also wrong.

III

Each day with its own marvel,
I wondered if he still remembers that am only his tenant and not his boss.
He further gave me another shocker,
My buckets are always filled with water awaiting my arrival from work by my Landlord
Every attempt to sweep my passage is always being cut short by his relations
Oh! what a Landlord.

IV

Is he truly a Landlord?
I've not recovered from this shock,
When one Sunday afternoon,
I was confronted with a bowl of exotic white Rice,
Courtesy of my Landlord and his wife,
Is this a Landlord?
Could someone provide me with an answer?
Where did I know this son of Adam from?
Are we from the same tribe? No.

Was I using charm on him? I don't think so,
Then why all this show of love, care and affection?
His Landlordship is quite different from the traditional Landlordship.

V

The greatest shocker came,
When we all fell casualties of the Bukuru crisis in Jos,
As a bachelor I ate outside,
Unfortunately, my sulphate finished a day before the crisis began,
Worse still, I only had my T.P. to office the next day,
With the intention of using any ATM.
Amazingly, this is the fourth day of the crisis, with twenty-four hours curfew,
How have I been feeding?
Who has been meeting my daily needs?
My Landlord and his family,
They provided breakfast and lunch regularly,
Is this part of my house rent?

VI

Oh! what a Landlord,
One more shocker,
He gave me Two Thousand Naira in the midst of the crisis to meet my other needs,
Is there no one to provide me with an answer?
Is this a Landlord?
How do I describe our relationship?
Did I say the greatest shocker?
How am I sure greater shocker would not come?
There are Landlords,
And there are Landlords,
But I met a Landlord with a difference,
God bless my Landlord.

FREEDOM

Freedom is not the absence of law and restriction,
For freedom without law is anarchy.
Freedom is not the absence of work and obligation,
For freedom demands more work than oppression.
Freedom is not retiring from responsibilities,
For responsibility increases with freedom.
Freedom is not relaxation,
For true freedom is permission to work and fulfill your potential.
Freedom is not a vacation from earthly responsibilities
For freedom demands hard work.
Freedom is not freedom to be left alone,
For no greater burden than freedom,
No heavier load than freedom.
For true freedom is more costly and demanding, than any form of oppression.

KOOM AND THE KEY BOARD

Oh Brother Koom!
All of a sudden you are becoming a Star,
All eyes on you on the key board.
Handsome young man,
Your posture and smiles on the keyboard angelic,
You are thrilling me,
You are becoming 'mamakious',
Keep it up!
Go for perfection,
The sky is not your limit,
If only you will fight the stardom spirit,
So many desire to have you,
Watch out!
Laugh! Laugh!! Laugh!!!

SELECTIVE JUSTICE

Why the selective justice?
Why are rules administered on just a few and not all?
Did they not say,
What is good for the Geese is good for the Gander?
What a shame.
When superior officers can no longer stand by their words,
Why give a query and deny the knowledge of such?
Why appear powerful on some and speechless over others?
For how long will this selective justice continue?
Though we appear not to have a god father,
But we have God as our father,
The father of justice and equity,
I call on you,
He will deliver us from jungle justice.
He will deliver us from the operators of jungle justice,
May they have a taste of this same selective justice,
Come quickly!

Come quickly!!
Deliver us from selective justice.

THE MIRACLE BUDGET

As the eyes of the Servant look unto his Master,
So, our eyes are on the Budget.
As the eyes of the Maiden look unto her Mistress,
So, our eyes are on the Budget.
The Miracle Budget,
The most controversial Budget,
The Miracle Budget,
The hope of the Masses,
The Miracle Budget,
The solution to all our problems,
The Miracle Budget,
The master key of the Ruling Party,
All eyes on the Miracle Budget,
Everyone anxiously waiting for the Presidential assent.

Why the fuel scarcity?
Wait for the Budget.

Why the hike in food prices?
Wait for the Budget.
Why the fall in power generation?
Wait for the Budget.
Why is our economy nose-diving?
Wait for the Budget.
Why so many abandoned road projects?
Wait for the Budget.
Why are our "Girls" not back?
Wait for the Budget.
Why is our Naira plummeting?
Wait for the Budget.

Why is the fight against corruption so slow?
Wait for the Budget.
Why the sudden unrest in our campuses?
Wait for the Budget.
Why are our men no longer performing their duties at home?
Wait for the Budget.
Why are our wives becoming so violent at home?
Wait for the Budget.
Everybody, waiting for the Budget.
The Miracle Budget indeed!
Come, Miracle Budget, Come!
The Messiah Miracle Budget Come!
Maranatha, Miracle Budget!
Will the Miracle Budget truly solve all our problems?

MY COUNTRY MY COUNTRY!!!

I

I woke up one morning
With my country on my mind,
What is it my beloved Country?
Each day has an interesting story of its own,
Stories to be cooked and dished by news makers,
From unimaginable tales to fallacies,
Some stories leave you confused and dumb founded,
Others too real to be false,
That's my Country for you,
My Country! My Country!

II

I woke up one morning,
With my country on my mind,
What is it again my beloved country?
Behold my new President,
My President a philosopher,

I am for everybody,
I am for nobody.
What does it really mean?
Watch out!
My Country! My Country!

III

I woke up one morning,
With my country on my mind,
What is it again my beloved Country?
It is the BBOG,
The vibrant and never quiet group,
Is gradually becoming dumb,
Are our girls back?
What has happened?
Has the tide changed?
My Country! My Country!

IV

I woke up one morning,
With my country on my mind,
What is it again my beloved Country?
It is the Dasukigate.
The human ATM,
Dispensed cash for over four years without network failure,
Pays a man over Billions of Naira for spiritual assignment,
Is it justifiable?
This is only possible in my beloved country.

My Country! My Country!

V

I woke up one morning,
With my country on my mind,
What is it again my beloved Country?
Boko Haram has been defeated technically,
But Boko Boys are still spilling innocent blood,
It doesn't matter,
We are winning the war,
Hahaha......
My Country! My Country!

VI

I woke up one morning,
With my country on my mind,
What is it again my beloved Country?
It is the change vocabulary,
Inconclusive Elections,
Kogi election-Inconclusive,
Rivers election-Inconclusive,
Bayelsa election-Inconclusive,
FCT election-Inconclusive,
Only in my beloved country,
My Country! My Country!

VII

I woke up one morning,
With my country on my mind,
What is it again my beloved Country?
It is the missing budget saga?
No not missing budget but padded budget,
No not padded budget but corrected budget,
No not corrected budget but smuggled budget,
What a shame!
My Country! My Country!

VIII

I woke up one morning,
With my country on my mind,
What is it again my beloved Country?
It is the Pep Guardiola Of Africa?
The African Guardiola that never was,
The Guardiola that saw tomorrow and took to his heels,
Three Matches,
Three Coaches,
Three Captains,
Three Goalkeepers,
Yet, we failed to qualify,
My Country! My Country!

IX

I woke up one morning,
With my country on my mind,
What is it again my beloved Country?
The saga of unbundling?
Some say restructuring,
Others say reengineering,
Then came the bomb,
I am not a magician.
My Country! My Country!

X

I woke up one morning,
With my country on my mind,
What is it again my beloved Country?
The almighty Panama Papers,
Panama the friend of the rich,
Panama the revealer of secrets,

Almighty Panama we hail you.
While some have resigned because of Panama,
Others are questioning the authenticity of Panama,
Oh! God help my beloved Country,
My Country! My Country!

COVID 19 LOCKDOWN

Citizens lock down
World economy shut down
National Economy weighed down
Spousal emotional breakdown
Personal finances melt down
Fear of job scale down
Anxiety over take-home slash down
The rich and the poor break down
Lock down offenders clamp down
Some innocent lives cut down
Prolong lock down may lead to show down
Tempers need to calm down
Very soon it will be count down
We will all say goodbye to Covid 19 Lockdown

ODE TO MY DG

DGs have come and gone
But you have been able to meander your way into the hearts of staff
Our jar of oil has never run dried since your arrival
We thought it was a fluke
But you proved us wrong
It has remained consistent
And it is getting better by the year
Oh! God bless my DG

DGs have come and gone
Some alive but are forgotten
But you came and perpetuated your name in gold
Beyond the hearts of staff
Upon the hearts of our families
Everyone looks forward to festive seasons
Always accompanied with special DG's gift
Oh! God bless my DG

DGs have come and gone
But your name remains fresh on the lips of our families
Our wives look forward to every festive season
Our children are too sure we will come back with DG's oil
Our neighbours are also beneficiaries of your magnanimity
Our parents from distant shores feel the warmth of your generousity
The DG with the heart of gold
Oh! God bless my DG-Mallam Yakubu Ibn Mohammed.

EPILOGUE

Most people dislike poetry because it is difficult to comprehend. Even moden day poets have not helped matters as they make poetry even more mysterious. Why can't a market woman read, comprehend and appreciate poetry? Why can't a road side mechanic pick up a book of poetry, read, comprehend and appreciate poetry? It is against this backdrop that I have decided to demystify the myth of making poetry elitist and difficult to comprehend. I want the ordinary man or woman on the street to identify with my kind of poetry. This collection RIVALRY OF SUPREMACY: A NEW APPROACH TO ENJOYING POETRY is simply my reflections, experiences about life and the task I have placed on my creative ingenuity to create something, either out of nothing or something. The most important thing for me is to document my thoughts, feelings and experiences as much as possible. In doing this, I try to give them wings to fly using poetry as the platform.

ACKNOWLEDGEMENT

With deep sense of gratitude to the almighty God who has made this work possible.

I want to sincerely thank my beloved wife Enny for tolerating my noisy soliloquy whenever am at the writing table. I say a million thank you. And to my angels Joan and Jessica, I love you.

I appreciate Hon. Terna Kester Kyenge for writing the foreword despite his busy schedules. May yourr literary ink never stop flowing.

Words are not enough to register my appreciation to Mrs. Mary Igboyi (Big aunty) who is always there for me. also, thank you ma for your suggestions towards making this book a success.

How can I forget Engr. Roy Ijogi and Engr. Hakeem Bello who were the first to look at my manuscripts. Thank you guys for comments and constructive criticisms. Engineers with literary minds.

My appreciation also goes to Noah Akanni (Irumole Kekere) for processing the ISBN. God bless you.

Furthermore, I would like to thank and express my heartfelt gratitude to the management of Programes Directorate, Nigerian Television Authority (NTA) Headquarters Abuja for their love and support especially Mr. Wole Coker Executive Director Programes for providing the atmosphere for creativity to thrive. I appreciate your wealth of experience sir.

Next I wish to thank my friends and colleagues- Miriam Gumwesh, Suleiman Usman, Oyinlola Alabi, Emeka Nguluka, Alex Omanchi, Olatunbosun Fagbemi and Dooshima Ikerave. Others ar Bayo Ogori, Elizabeth Agbai, Thelma Obaze, patience Abah, Magdalene Aikhonmu, Susan Adamu, Soaga Mubasheer, Umma Umar, Ene Onobu, Maryann Ayana, Christy Akpasoh, Sembene Oculi, Kachi Ogba and Ishaya Bulus. I celebrate you all.

Above all, to my DG. Mal. Yakubu Ibn Mohammed, I admire your sterling leadership qualities and your concern towards staff welfare. God bless you sir.

Finally, to all those who have contributed towards my success in life in one way or the other but whom space would not permit me to mention their names, God will grant you your heart desires.

See you at the top!

ABOUT THE AUTHOR

Francis A.ogbe

Francis A. Ogbe a passionate TV Producer, Creative TV Director, Quintessential Scriptwriter and a meticulous Transmission Director is a producer with Nigerian Television Authority. (NTA) Headquarters Abuja. He has produced programmes like The Environment, Food Today, AM Express and Wellbeing on the network service of NTA. He is an integral part of one of the flagship programmes on NTA called Weekend Deal- a weekly breakfast show that has become viewers delight. He hold a BA (Hons) Drama and Masters of Art Degree in Drama from the prestigious Ahmadu Bello University (ABU) Zaria and a Post Graduate Diploma in Education.

BOOKS BY THIS AUTHOR

Catch Them Young: Discovering New Ways To Meeting The Needs Of Today's Youths

You would learn and discover the following from this time bomb-book

* What the whole concept of christotainment is all about
* Whether it is right or wrong for youths to celebrate valentine
* The secrets to discovering and displaying your gifts
* One thing God will never do for man
* Whether youths of opposite sex can be friends without flirting
* How to sow viable seeds at the youthful season in order to reap greatness at old age
* How to make your dream a reality

Let My People Go: How To Win The Battle Of The Mind

Spiritual warfare is all about the battle of the mind. Whoever controls your mind controls your wife. The weapons of our warfare are meant to do three things:

1. Pulling down strongholds
2. Casting down imaginations
3. Bringing into captivity every thought

What are strongholds? Strongholds are wrong belief system, ideologies and wrong convictions. Where does imagination takes place? In the mind! Where do thoughts take place? In the mind! It is therefore crystal clear that spiritual warefare is all about the control of the mind. It is a mind game.

Our greatest undoing as believers is not the devil but ignorance of our enviable position in Christ Jesus. Therefore, your mentality must change. You cannot carry a defeatist mentality around and expect Pharaoh to let you go. As a man thinketh in his heart so is he.

www.ingramcontent.com/pod-product-compliance
Lightning Source LLC
La Vergne TN
LVHW050600160826
845677LV00011B/2388